myinspiredlife

Love Notes Journal
for our
Wedding Anniversary

Inspired Life
PRESS

National Library of Australia

Cataloguing-in-Publication entry:

Hilton, Ayesha (1973)

Love Notes Journal for our Wedding Anniversary

1st ed.

ISBN: 978-0-9944229-5-8 (paperback)

Journal, Wedding, Anniversary

Interior & Cover Images: Pixabay

Published by Inspired Life Press
Email: info@InspiredLifePress.com

To see other titles published by Inspired Life Press visit:
www.InspiredLifePress.com

Celebrating Our Marriage

Date: _____

Husband: _____
&
Wife: _____

Celebrate Your Wedding Anniversary with this Journal

Whether you are newly weds, or you've been married for decades, it is important to show your love and appreciation for each other. In our busy lives, we can easily take each other for granted.

On your anniversary, rather than writing a card, you can use this journal to write a love note to each other. Over the years, you will be creating a beautiful keepsake of your marriage that you can treasure.

Set aside time to reflect and celebrate the year that has just passed. Take note of the good times and also the challenges that you have overcome together.

And if you go through tough times, as we all do from time to time, get out this journal and look through it and remember why you fell in love and how much you have meant to each other.

Allow this journal to keep the fires of love that has been lost between you and for it to strengthen your commitment to each other.

I hope this anniversary journal will become a book of celebration of your love over the years.

I wish you many years of happiness, joy, abundance, good health, and lots of laughter.

With love and best wishes,

Ayesha Hilton

Check out our other great journals & coloring books!

myinspiredlife.club

About Our Engagement

Stick a photo here if you like.

When: _____

Where: _____

About our Engagement:

_____

_____

_____

_____

_____

_____

_____

_____

_____

_____

_____

_____

_____

_____

_____

About Our Wedding

Stick a photo here if you like.

When: _____

Where: _____

About our wedding:

_____

_____

_____

_____

_____

_____

_____

_____

_____

_____

_____

_____

_____

Every love story
is beautiful,
But ours is my
favourite!

My Husband
What I LOVE about you

My Wife
What I LOVE about you

I can't promise I can fix
all your problems,
But I can promise you this:
you won't face them alone.

Celebrating Our Anniversary

Year:

This year, we celebrate our

Wedding Anniversary.

To My Husband on our Anniversary

Date:

To My Wife on our Anniversary

Date:

"You know when you're in love when you can't fall sleep because reality is finally better than your dreams."
Dr. Seuss

Celebrating Our Anniversary

Year: _____

This year, we celebrate our

_____

Wedding Anniversary.

To My Husband on our Anniversary

Date:

To My Wife on our Anniversary

Date:

I promise to remember that
neither of us is perfect.
But I will strive to remind
myself of the ways we are
perfect for each other.

Celebrating Our Anniversary

Year:

This year, we celebrate our

Wedding Anniversary.

To My Husband on our Anniversary

Date:

To My Wife on our Anniversary

Date:

The good things in life
are better with you!

Celebrating Our Anniversary

Year:

This year, we celebrate our

Wedding Anniversary.

To My Husband on our Anniversary

Date:

To My Wife on our Anniversary

Date:

I not only love you for
who you are,
but for who I am
when I am with you.

Celebrating Our Anniversary

Year:

This year, we celebrate our

Wedding Anniversary.

To My Husband on our Anniversary

Date:

To My Wife on our Anniversary

Date:

I choose to spend my life with you.

And I'll continue to choose you,
over and over.

Celebrating Our Anniversary

Year:

This year, we celebrate our

Wedding Anniversary.

To My Husband on our Anniversary

Date: _____

To My Wife on our Anniversary

Date:

"The best love is the kind that
awakens the soul;
that makes us reach for more,
that plants the fire in our hearts
and brings peace to our minds.
That's what I hope to
give you forever."
The Notebook

Celebrating Our Anniversary

Year: _____

This year, we celebrate our

_____

Wedding Anniversary.

To My Husband on our Anniversary

Date:

To My Wife on our Anniversary

Date:

Thank you for sharing
your life with me

We bring out the best
in each other

Celebrating Our Anniversary

Year:

This year, we celebrate our

Wedding Anniversary.

To My Husband on our Anniversary

Date:

To My Wife on our Anniversary

Date:

"The greatest happiness of life is the conviction that we are loved; loved for ourselves, or rather, loved in spite of ourselves."
Victor Hugo

Celebrating Our Anniversary

Year:

This year, we celebrate our

Wedding Anniversary.

To My Husband on our Anniversary

Date:

To My Wife on our Anniversary

Date:

I love your smile
I love your eyes
I love your voice
I love your laugh
I love your soul

I Love You

Celebrating Our Anniversary

Year: [ ]

This year, we celebrate our

[ ]

Wedding Anniversary.

To My Husband on our Anniversary

Date:

To My Wife on our Anniversary

Date:

Thank you for the magic
and the moonlight.

For the kisses and the cuddles.

For dreams and reality
all mixed in together.

myinspiredlife.club

Printed in the USA
CPSIA information can be obtained
at www.ICGtesting.com
LVHW070714260823
756374LV00051B/1737